Dedication

It is with great love that we dedicate this course to Polly Wyant Thomas. Every day, this woman came before the throne of the Almighty King, praying for the staff, board and class members of ZOE Ministries International. Her vision for this ministry went beyond what the normal eye could see. Polly's tenacity before the throne was awe-inspiring. She was similar to Anna, the New Testament prophetess, who "never left the temple but worshiped night and day, fasting and praying."

We greatly miss our precious Polly and her love for intercession on behalf of ZOE. However, we do know that she is now enjoying the beautiful presence of the Lord she knew so well here on earth. We thank You, Jesus, for giving us Polly!

3

Acknowledgments

ZOE Ministries International equips, trains and sends believers into the world to minister by the leading of the Holy Spirit. This dedicated ministry encourages God's people to use their gifts and talents in building the body of Christ for His glory. For that purpose, and with the Holy Spirit's leading, ZOE Ministries compiled this study guide. We wish to thank many faithful individuals for their support, time and talents, and to give our Lord all the praise and glory for this work!

Who Is Jesus?

Encounters With The Real Jesus

PART 1

OF

CAPTIVATED

BY THEIR

CHARACTER

WHO IS JESUS?

About This Study

Who Is Jesus? is Part One of a three-part study on the Trinity titled *Captivated by Their Character.*

Captivated by Their Character is designed to enrich your understanding of who God is—His character, His desires and plans. As you proceed through this Study Guide, you will examine what God says about Himself in the Bible. May God show you some glimpses of Himself as Father, Son and Holy Spirit.

Captivated by Their Character attempts to do the impossible! It tries to explain an invisible, dynamic God, who has revealed Himself to us humans as three persons. Although our finite minds may never fully plumb the depths of the mystery of God's full identity, we can gather some clues. The three different parts in the study correspond to the three members of the Trinity. We suggest that you proceed through them in the arranged order—*Who Is Jesus, Who Is God the Father, Who Is the Holy Spirit.* Each part contains six lessons.

Each lesson in *Who Is Jesus* begins with an introduction or story. Specific Bible verses and corresponding questions follow. May you come to know His complete goodness and passionate love for you.

For Self-Study

All that is required for this study is a Bible and an inquiring heart. After you read the questions posed in each lesson, record your response to the questions in the space provided or in a separate journal. We trust that as you meditate on the verses, God will, over time, draw you into an even closer relationship with Him.

For Lesson 6, you will find an additional Facilitator's Version at the back of the book. For this lesson, we suggest that you complete the regular lesson by reading the scriptures listed and prayerfully answering the questions on your own. When you are finished, you can read the Facilitator's Version to perhaps gain new understanding.

For Use in a Small Group

For guidance in using this study in a small group setting, see the Leader's Guide section found in the back of this book. There is a Facilitator's Version of Lesson 6 for your use, located after the Leader's Guide.

Foreword

Has the subject of the Trinity ever brought confusion and frustration? The Father, Son and Holy Spirit are uniquely the same, and yet they have different roles. During this part of the study you will have the opportunity to examine what the Bible says about one person of the Trinity—Jesus, the Son.

Out of God's great love for the world, He sent His one and only Son as a living sacrifice in order to bring mankind back into relationship with Himself. Jesus, out of love and obedience to His Father, came to earth to fulfill God's plan and offered Himself as the once and for all sacrifice.

Before Jesus' death, He told His disciples that He would send the Holy Spirit to live in them and be with them forever. After Jesus' resurrection, the Father sent the Holy Spirit to live in all people who believe in Jesus as Lord. We would be totally "lost" without the Holy Spirit's presence in our lives.

The Trinity, three in one, may be a mystery; however, upon studying each person in the Trinity, we firmly believe that you will be *captivated by their character.* Our prayer is that God, by His Holy Spirit, will teach you all things, for His glory!

Dick and Ginny Chanda
Founding Directors
ZOE Ministries International

"In the beginning was the Word, and the Word was with God, and the Word was God ...In Him was life [zoe], and that life [zoe] was the light of men."   *John 1:1, 4*

"I am the way and the truth and the life. No one comes to the Father except through me."
                                                  John 14:6

WHO IS JESUS?   Jesus is the Word! Jesus is life! Jesus is light! This course introduces you to Jesus as the Word, who comes to life and shines forth light by which to live! Come get acquainted with Jesus and see how He relates to people as individuals.

For Self-Study
- You will need a Bible for this course. As you proceed through each lesson, prayerfully read the scriptures listed and record your response to the questions in the space provided.

- There are two versions for Lesson 6. We suggest that you complete the regular version, answering the questions on your own. When you are finished, you can read the Facilitator's Version in the back of the book to perhaps gain new understanding.

13

For Use in a Small Group
- Please refer to the "Leader's Guide" section at the back of this book for guidance in leading/facilitating this course.

- Each lesson is designed to last one hour.

- This course is designed to last six weeks. You may want to extend the course, if needed.

- Each participant will need a copy of this Study Guide, or you may copy the pages containing the questions, to give to participants.

- It is helpful to hand out copies of the same version of the Bible. Then participants can turn to a specific page number, making it easy for them to find a passage.

THE RICH YOUNG RULER   Mark 10:17–27

Jesus related and responded to many people during His 33 years on earth and we can learn much about who He is from these encounters. We learn of His ways by observing how He treated each individual uniquely. He called them forth from their life as it was to a new level of living. Our study today is unique in that this person chose *not* to accept the call.

We don't know much about this man's background, hometown or occupation. We are told in Matthew's account of this man that he was young. Youth is often characterized by abundant energy and enthusiasm. We read that this man ran up to Jesus, fell on his knees and started talking, all of which show his youthful enthusiasm. Luke's account of this story says the man was a "ruler," meaning he was probably a member of some official court or council, but we don't know what he ruled over. Another detail we know is that he was very wealthy. Perhaps he had inherited his wealth or maybe he was simply a very successful businessman.

We can also tell that this young, rich fellow was also quite religious. No doubt he was a good Jew, saying and doing all that the Law of Moses required. He was probably raised in a God-fearing home by parents who diligently taught him the difference between right and wrong. Yet underneath all his zeal and devotion we can detect that he knew something was missing. All of his ritual obedience to the many rules and regulations was not getting him closer to eternal life. *There's got to be more, he thought.*

Jesus was a recognized teacher in Israel with a significant group of followers. There was much talk about Him and many reports of the miracles He did. Nobody could refute the authority and power in this man. He wasn't merely a good teacher saying wonderful things. When He spoke, things happened! What kind of person was this? Maybe, just maybe, Jesus could help the rich young ruler with his quest for eternal life. Turn to **Mark 10:17–27** to read of their encounter.

Discussion Questions

1. What did the rich young ruler ask Jesus? What does his question show about *how* he hoped to get this eternal life?

2. What do you think Jesus was looking for in this person when He said, "Obey the commandments"?

3. Not satisfied with that answer, the young man declared his own obedience to the law since childhood. Next we read that Jesus looked at him and *loved* him. What prompted this love response?

What did He see in this individual?

_____

_____

_____

4. In effect, Jesus said, "Good job! There is one more thing you need to do! Go, sell..." Why did Jesus call this person to such a great sacrifice?

_____

_____

_____

5. What was the main obstacle in this person's pursuit of the kingdom of God?

_____

_____

_____

6. Can a rich person have eternal life? Does Jesus condemn wealth?

_____

_____

_____

7. Why did Jesus say it is hard for the rich to enter the kingdom of God?

_____

_____

_____

_____

8. How does one enter the kingdom of God? Read **Titus 3:4–5**.

Considering Christ

The rich young ruler's facial expression suddenly became sad and he turned and left. All of his youthful enthusiasm had been drained away. Jesus' invitation to eternal life exposed the real obstacle that kept him from being saved. He came wanting something to *do*. Jesus showed that it wasn't in doing but rather in receiving by faith that we are saved. It is God's job to save us; our part is believing and receiving Jesus.

Jesus addresses several hindrances to salvation in the parable of the sower. Read **Mark 4:1–20.** What kind of soil would you say the rich young ruler was?

Hebrews 13:5 says, "Keep your lives free from the love of money and be content with what you have, because God has said, 'Never will I leave you; never will I forsake you.' " How can we keep our lives from being choked by the love of money?

Jesus never condemned riches or wealth but He cautioned us that it is often easy to forget what is important when riches are involved. He wants our undivided love and loyalty. Read **Matthew 6:19–21**. Where is your treasure?

THE SORROWING WOMAN   Luke 7:11–17

The two crowds met on the steep slope of a hill near the gates of the city of Nain. They were located six miles from Jesus' hometown of Nazareth. The view was wide across the plains. They could see the snowy heights of Mount Hermon on the horizon.

Jesus and a large number of His disciples climbed up the hill, as the other group moved down the hill toward the rock-hewn tombs that lined the eastern side of the road. The latter group was led by mourners, whose shrieks and lamentations pierced the air.

In the middle of the procession, relatives and friends moved slowly under the weight of a young man on an open bier. The dead man's mother walked beside the stretcher, weeping. She was a widow, and now she had lost her only son.

The birth of this son had been an occasion for great celebration. In the Jewish culture, giving birth to a son gave a woman value in her husband's eyes. A baby boy ensured the hope of passing on the family wealth and name. His presence was guaranteed security in old age. It would be his responsibility to care for his aging parents, and especially for his widowed mother.

It was thus the hope of every Jewish woman to have a son, and God had granted this woman that desire. But now...she was left utterly alone. Already she had suffered her husband's death, and now her only son's. She knew, as did those who followed her to the burial caves, that the future held only the grim prospect of destitute dependence upon the mercy of friends and strangers.

As the widow and the procession of mourners were leaving the city gate, just then Jesus and His disciples reached the top of the hill and the city's entrance. Totally of His own initiative, Jesus came alongside to talk to her.

What happened next astounded the widow and the crowd that followed her. No one would have believed it if they hadn't observed the incident with their own eyes. In fact, news of it spread like wildfire through the entire region. People whispered to each other in fearful and awed tones. Soon there wasn't a household in the district that wasn't discussing Jesus and what He had done.

Read **Luke 7:11–17** and consider these questions as you discover the conclusion to this story.

Discussion Questions

1. Read **Luke 7:12–13** again. Try to imagine what the widow might have been feeling.

2. What motivated Jesus to approach the widow? (**verse 13**).

3. In this scene, what action did Jesus take? (**verses 14–15**).

4. If you had been the widow, how would you have responded to what Jesus said and did?

5. What was the crowd's response to this miracle? (**verse 16**)

6. Judging from what you have seen in this encounter, how would you describe Christ? What kind of person is He?

7. Have you ever had a loss or disappointment so shattering that you felt you wouldn't recover?

Considering Christ

Jesus saw this individual's need and compassionately reached out to help her. He seemed acutely aware of her pain and more than willing to help.

Here is another short, perhaps familiar passage from Matthew's Gospel in which Jesus Himself states His willingness to lift our load. What does Christ promise to give those who carry heavy burdens?

> "Come to me, all you who are weary and burdened, and I will give you rest. Take my yoke upon you and learn from me, for I am gentle and humble in heart, and you will find rest for your souls. For my yoke is easy and my burden is light." *Matthew 11:28–30*

> He said, "Surely they are my people . . ."; and so He became their Savior. In all their distress He too was distressed. *Isaiah 63:8–9*

Reprinted with permission from NavPress.

∼ THE ADULTEROUS WOMAN   John 8:2–11

At the height of Christ's ministry, the people followed Him every-
where He went. His popularity, however, was an increasing threat to
the Jewish leaders. They searched for a way to discredit Him. The
person who is the subject of this study presented the golden opportunity to do so—or so they thought.

On this particular occasion, Jesus appeared in the Temple courts
at dawn. There was still a chill in the air, and the sky was streaked
with red. People gathered around Him, and soon He sat down and
began to teach.

Suddenly angry voices interrupted His lesson. The scribes and
the Pharisees (the Jewish religious leaders) elbowed their way to the
front like a vigilante squad, dragging a disheveled woman with them.

Shoving her in front of Jesus, they shouted out her sin for all
to hear. "Teacher," they said, "this woman was caught in the act of
adultery. In the Law Moses commanded us to stone such women.
Now what do you say?"

Here, then, was the trap they had waited for, and this woman was merely the bait. If Jesus said to let her go, then He would be guilty of rejecting the Old Testament Law. If He told the scribes and Pharisees to stone her, then the crowd would claim He was no longer a sympathetic friend of common people. He would also be challenging Roman law, which did not allow the Jews to carry out the death sentence.

As this woman stood in front of Jesus with the hostile crowd behind her, she must have been terrified. Death by stoning was painful and prolonged, and that ordeal might well be hers within the hour.

She watched Jesus bend down from where He sat and begin tracing something on the ground in front of her. The accusing voices grew louder and more insistent. At last Jesus straightened up, looked directly at the men, and spoke.

To find out what Jesus said, and how this story ends, read and consider this scene in **John 8:2–11**.

Discussion Questions

1. How did the scribes and Pharisees treat this woman?

2. What guilty party was strangely missing from this scene?

3. What emotions did this woman probably experience during this dramatic encounter?

4. Why did the scribes and Pharisees leave when Jesus said, "If any-one of you is without sin, let him be the first to throw a stone at her"? (**John 8:7–9**)

5. Why do you think she stayed, even after her accusers had gone? Why didn't she just slip off when the crowd left?

6. Who is the one who had the right to accuse her? (**John 8:46–47**)

7. How would you describe the way Jesus treated this person?

8. What motivated Jesus to forgive her? (**John 3:16–17**)

9. Since all those in the crowd were confronted with their sin, why was this individual the only one Jesus forgave?

    _____

    _____

    _____

10. Think about Christ's final words to her. How was this person's new life to be different from her life before?

    _____

    _____

    _____

Considering Christ

As this scene closes, the spotlight lingers on the two key figures: Jesus and the woman who was caught in adultery. Her sin, committed in private, was made public by men not a whit more righteous than she. Yet here she stood—forgiven, protected, and secure in the presence of the only one who could have justly condemned her. Ironically, she was able to take refuge in Christ only because her dark, hidden secrets had been exposed ...and forgiven.

We all long for a similar sense of safety and security. But to experience that kind of spiritual refuge, we, too, must be willing to look honestly at ourselves and to turn from our sin. When the Bible uses the word "sin," it is speaking of the basic tendency we each have to go our own way, to do our own thing.

If the secrets of our hearts were laid open and bare before a holy God, what would He see? What would we see? In the book of **Romans**, there is a short passage that summarizes the predicament we find ourselves in apart from God's intervention. Read **Romans 3:10–12** and try putting these verses in your own words.

There is, thankfully, a more hopeful note following only a few chapters later. In **Romans 5:8**, what is that message of hope?

> **God, the heavenly parent, is love, and therefore He wants children upon whom He can lavish His love and receive their love in return.**
> *E. Stanley Jones*

> **(Jesus) loves us and has freed us from our sins by His blood...** *Revelation 1:5*

Reprinted with permission from NavPress.

THE MILITARY MAN   Matthew 8:5–13

Jesus' encounter with the centurion took place in Capernaum, a flourishing seaside fishing village on the northwestern shore of the Sea of Galilee. Capernaum was located on a major international road that stretched from Damascus to the Mediterranean coast and on down to Egypt. Because of this location, it is reasonable to assume that there was significant traffic through this city. Interestingly, Capernaum was well below sea level because the Sea of Galilee is nearly 700 feet below sea level. It was here in Capernaum that Jesus found and called several of His disciples including Matthew, a tax collector, Andrew, a fisherman, and his brother Simon Peter. In fact, Peter's home in Capernaum became Jesus' base of operations during His time of ministry in Galilee.

Although we are never given the centurion's name, we do know some things about his occupation. A centurion was a Roman officer in charge of about 100 soldiers. Israel was under Roman rule and the centurions were part of the military network set up for keeping order. A Roman legion consisted of about 6,000 men divided into

10 regiments of 600 each. A centurion commanded 1/6 of a regiment; that is, 100 men. Centurions were carefully chosen because they provided necessary stability and support to the Roman Empire.

In addition to being in charge of 100 soldiers, this centurion also had servants in his home in Capernaum. On this day, one of his most valued servants was very sick and was suffering greatly. It was out of his concern and compassion that he looked for help. Perhaps he had first gone to the local doctors, seeking whatever aid they could offer, but it was to no avail. What should he do now? Time was of the essence or his servant might die.

Read **Matthew 8:5–13** to find out what happened next.

Discussion Questions

1. Why do you think the centurion went to find Jesus? What did he expect?

_____

_____

_____

_____

2. Jesus' response to the centurion's request was immediate, even though this man wasn't a Jew. Why was this? Do you think this caught the centurion off guard?

_____

_____

_____

_____

3. Note the centurion's response in **Matthew 8:8–9**. What does this show about his perception of Jesus?

_____

_____

4. Upon hearing the man's words, Jesus was astonished and amazed. Why? How could He tell that this person had great faith?

5. Jesus said to the man, "Go! It will be done just as you believed it would." What was the end result? How do you think the centurion's life was affected as a result of meeting Jesus?

6. It is often in those "crisis times" that we look to God and cry, "Help!" Has this ever happened to you?

Considering Christ

The Bible mentions that Jesus was "amazed" only two times. Read **Mark 6:1–6**. Here we read that Jesus was amazed at the *unbelief* of the people in Nazareth, the town He grew up in. In today's study we see Jesus amazed at the centurion's *faith*. In Nazareth, many, if not most, of the people knew of Jesus and His family. They could have observed His character in daily life, yet they didn't have faith in Him. Now in Capernaum, a Roman centurion, a Gentile and total stranger, shows great faith in Jesus.

It seems that sometimes being familiar with church and Jesus stuff can stand in the way and cause us to miss out on powerful encounters with God's love. Jesus said we should come to God like children—trusting and expectant. He will meet us, and our life can be forever changed by God's power!

THE WOMAN WHO WORSHIPED

Mark 14:1–9

Jesus Christ is so often pictured in the midst of crowds of people that we sometimes forget that He knew the pleasure of a quiet, intimate evening with close friends.

Mary and Martha and their brother, Lazarus, were some of those who knew the joy of His private company. They often entertained Jesus in their home. Martha orchestrated the dinner while Mary listened attentively to Jesus. In Christ's willingness to teach Mary, He defied the Jewish tradition that held that women need not be taught—indeed, they weren't capable of learning (**Luke 10:38–42**). Mary was drawn to this man who treated her with such respect. She was accepted and secure in His company.

In this scene, we find Jesus once again having dinner with Mary, Martha, and Lazarus—but this time in the home of Simon the leper. Christ had stopped in Bethany on His way to the great Jewish feast in Jerusalem, the Passover.

Jesus knew that this would be His final trip to Jerusalem. The opposition to His ministry was building. Yet strangely, His closest friends seemed oblivious to the confrontation sure to come—all of His friends, that is, except Mary.

Mary saw the significance of what was happening. This was not merely another pleasant evening spent with Jesus. Mary demonstrated her awareness of the events about to unfold, as well as her devotion to Jesus, by one extraordinary act.

Mary had good reason to express her gratitude to Jesus. At an earlier point, her brother Lazarus had become ill. She and her sister, Martha, sent for Christ, but by the time Jesus got there, Lazarus had been dead for four days. In a moving account in John's Gospel, Jesus raised Lazarus from the dead (**John 11:1–44**).

To see what Mary did, read **Mark 14:1–9**. (This passage speaks of an anonymous woman who, we learn from John's account of the same occasion, **John 12:1–8**, was Mary of Bethany.)

Discussion Questions

1. How would you describe the type of relationship Jesus had with Mary? (**John 11:5**)

2. What event was Mary thinking about as she anointed Him with this expensive perfume?

3. How much could Mary have sold the perfume for if she had lived today?

4. How did the men around Mary respond to what she did? How did Jesus respond?

5. What did Mary's action show about her devotion to the Lord Jesus?

Considering Christ

This scene foreshadows the crucifixion of Christ, which is the ultimate statement in all of God's communication with us. God, at last, became the Word that He spoke; that is, He took on human form and lived among us. And now we see Him on His way to being crucified in Jerusalem.

But what does His death really mean? What difference can it make to us as individuals? The Old Testament prophets spoke of the death of the Messiah, Jesus spoke of His own death, and later books in the New Testament explain even further its significance.

Consider these three major references as you seek to formulate your own conclusions about the crucifixion of Jesus Christ.

Isaiah 53:4–6

John 10:14–18

Colossians 2:13–14

> God demonstrates His own love for us in this:
> While we were still sinners, Christ died for us.
> ***Romans 5:8***

Reprinted with permission from NavPress.

WHO IS JESUS?
Participant's Version

1. "In the beginning was the Word, and the Word was with God, and the Word was God. He was with God in the beginning. Through Him all things were made; without Him nothing was made that has been made." *John 1:1–3*

   Genesis 1:1, 26 "In the beginning God created the heavens and the earth ...Then God said, 'Let us make man in our image, in our likeness... .' " *Genesis 1:1, 26*

   John 1:2 refers to a person ("**He**"). Who was with God in the beginning? What else do we learn from these verses?

   _____

   _____

   _____

   _____

2. **"...in whom we have redemption, the forgiveness of sins. He is the image of the invisible God, the firstborn over all creation. For by Him all things were created... ."**   *Colossians 1:14–16*

   This verse also refers to Jesus Christ as being involved in creation. What else do we learn about Jesus?

   _____

   _____

   _____

3. **"The Word became flesh and made His dwelling among us. We have seen His glory, the glory of the One and Only, who came from the Father, full of grace and truth."**
   John 1:14

   One of the names of Jesus is **"the Word."** Why is He called that? What does it mean?

   _____

   _____

   _____

   The term *word* here is defined as a "divine expression or communication of the inward thoughts and feelings of God."

   How is Jesus the divine expression or communication of the inward thoughts and feelings of God?

   _____

   _____

   _____

4. The Bible is called the Word of God. Compare these verses about Jesus, the Word, with the verses about the Word of God.

   "In Him [Jesus] was life, and that life was the light of men.

The light shines in the darkness, but the darkness has not understood it." *John 1:4–5*

"Jesus answered, 'I am the way and the truth and the life. No one comes to the Father except through me.' " *John 14:6*

"For the word of God is living and active." *Hebrews 4:12*

How is Jesus like the Word of God in these verses?

5. Now compare these verses about Jesus and the Word of God.

"When Jesus spoke again to the people, He said, 'I am the light of the world. Whoever follows me will never walk in darkness, but will have the light of life.' " *John 8:12*

"Your [God's] word is a lamp to my feet and a light for my path." *Psalm 119:105*

How is Jesus like the Word of God in these verses?

6. Some people assume that Jesus wrote the Scriptures, the Bible, but that is not true.

"Above all, you must understand that no prophecy of Scripture came about by the prophet's own interpretation. For prophecy never had its origin in the will of man, but men spoke from God as they were carried along by the

Holy Spirit."   *2 Peter 1:20–21*

"All Scripture is God-breathed... ."   *2 Timothy 3:16*

According to these verses, who did write the Scriptures?

Jesus said, **"Heaven and earth will pass away, but my words will never pass away" (Matthew 24:35).** See **Matthew 5:18** and **Psalms 119:89** for further study.

7. Why do you think that the Bible is difficult to understand at times?

"This is what we speak, not in words taught us by human wisdom but in words taught by the Spirit, expressing spiritual truths in spiritual words. The man without the Spirit does not accept the things that come from the Spirit of God, for they are foolishness to him, and he cannot understand them, because they are spiritually discerned."
1 Corinthians 2:13–14

8. Why do you think the Scriptures (the Bible) were written?

"But these are written that you may believe that Jesus is the Christ, the son of God, and that by believing you may have life in His name." *John 20:31*

To further develop your relationship with God, we recommend the following courses offered by ZOE Ministries International.

For new believers, we recommend completing the Who Is Jesus?, Who Is God the Father?, Who Is the Holy Spirit? and Hearing God's Voice courses before taking other ZOE courses.

Who Is Jesus?
Jesus is the Word! Jesus is life! Jesus is light! This course introduces you to Jesus as the Word, who comes to life and shines forth light by which to live! Come get acquainted with Jesus and see how He relates to people as individuals.

Who Is God the Father?
The Lord is gracious. He is compassionate! He is slow to anger! He is rich in love! (Psalm 145:8) This course introduces you to God the Father, who comes to life and displays His love and generosity. Come get acquainted with God as Father and see how He relates to us, His children.

Who Is the Holy Spirit?
He is the Counselor, Comforter and Helper! He teaches and guides us! The Father sent Him to be with us permanently.
This course introduces you to the Holy Spirit, who comes to life and empowers us to become more like Jesus. Come get acquainted with the Holy Spirit and see how He relates to us as our Helper.

HEARING COURSES

Hearing God's Voice

In this course, everyone is encouraged to participate by applying the principles they read in scripture in order to learn to recognize when the Holy Spirit is speaking. The inner knowing, inner voice, and the authoritative voice of the Holy Spirit are discussed, as well as other manifestations of the Holy Spirit. The Lord is personal and unique, and desires to communicate with each one of His sheep in a personal and unique manner! (This course is a prerequisite for all the following courses except for *How to Hear God's Voice—In Marriage*.)

How to Hear God's Voice—In Christ

In the *Hearing God's Voice* course we learned how to hear God as individuals, whereas in the In Christ course, we learn how the body of Christ operates together under His direction and to His glory. We look at Romans 12 and examine the motive gifts that determine our individual bents. This study enables us to understand, appreciate and love each other. We also look at the Trinity and how they operate together. We learn about the precious person of the Holy Spirit and how He teaches, guides and comforts us. We also learn about the gifts of the Holy Spirit in 1 Corinthians 12 and 14 brought about as the Holy Spirit moves through us. Participants have remarked that this course has enabled them to see people the way God sees them and how they fit in the body of Christ.

How to Hear God's Voice—In Marriage

This course is based on the love relationship God had with mankind in the very beginning. We examine our attitudes toward each other and how they reflect the greatest love of all, the love of Christ. Do we love and honor each other with the unconditional love that our Lord Jesus had for us while dying on the cross? As in previous courses, we examine scripture, seek the Lord, and ask

Him, "How can I better serve and love my spouse?" We discover how we complete each other, not compete with each other.

How to Hear God's Voice—In Family

In today's society we see the growing deterioration of the family. Parents are confused about what the Bible teaches on family issues. During this course we examine scriptures and what it means to: "Train up a child [early childhood] in the way he should go [and in keeping with his individual bent], and when he is old [teen years can be the best] he will not depart from it." (AMP with additions)

http://www.zoeministries.org/hearing-gods-voice/

KNOWING COURSES

How to Know God's Voice—In Intimate Friendship

Intimate Friendship with God! Can we experience such a relationship with the Creator of the universe? Here we examine what the Bible teaches us about the fear of the Lord, and how we can, indeed, have a deeper, more intimate relationship with Him. This is a very personal, yet freeing course on growing intimacy with God.

How to Know God's Voice—In Worship

The focus of this course is on ministering to the Lord. During our time together the Lord draws us corporately into His presence as we worship Him. We study what worship is, why we worship, and how we worship.

How to Know God's Voice—In His Presence

The Lord is calling each one of His sheep to come into His presence and to know Him in a deeper way. This course is not for the new believer nor the faint in heart. Those who are serious about knowing the Father in a more intimate way will find this course challenging but rewarding. Examining Jesus' last days on earth will direct us into the presence of the Lord. This course is for those who have completed other ZOE courses.

How to Know God's Voice—In the Coming of the Lord
Many are proclaiming dates and times when the Lord Jesus will return for His bride. This course is designed to focus on our preparation for His coming, not when He is coming, and to better understand the Lord's statement of Revelation 22:20: "Yes, I am coming." It is the goal of this course to prepare ourselves as the bride of Christ, with hearts that will respond with "Amen. Come, Lord Jesus."

http://www.zoeministries.org/knowing-gods-voice/

FOLLOWING COURSES

How to Follow God's Voice—In Healing

During this course we examine the scriptures in which Jesus healed the sick. The Holy Spirit highlights these passages as we study, and our faith increases! We realize that Jesus is the Healer, and we are simply His vessels as we listen to and follow His voice.

How to Follow God's Voice—In Power
Evangelism is often thought of as a bad word! In this course we come to realize that God has a special plan for evangelism for us if we are only sensitive and obedient to His voice. Preparing your testimony, leading someone in salvation, and discipling others are a few of the topics discussed in this course. This is a real life-changer as we minister in "power evangelism!"

How to Follow God's Voice—In Intercession
Jesus is in constant intercession (Hebrews 7:25). As we come before Him in worship, intercession is a natural outflow of our relationship with Him. By yielding to the Holy Spirit, our ministry to others

through intercession will increase.

How to Follow God's Voice—In Spiritual Warfare
As we come to know and recognize who our Lord is, He reveals to us who He is not! The tactics of Satan and our spiritual weapons are defined in this course. The Lord leads us in spiritual warfare as He enlists and mobilizes His army!

http://www.zoeministries.org/following-gods-voice/

ONE-ON-ONE DISCIPLESHIP

Discipleship by the Word of God and the Power of the Holy Spirit.

This 12-week course was developed by a disciple-maker after many years of successful one-on-one discipleship. Through this method the Holy Spirit is allowed to minister to the disciple through the Word and the encouragement of the disciple-maker. No other techniques or methods are used.

The entire course has been designed to enable individuals to feel confident in making disciples as directed by our Lord: *"Therefore go and make disciples of all nations ...."* Matthew 28:19.

Not only do the participants learn what discipleship means according to the Word of God, but they are encouraged to participate in a one-on-one discipleship program as part of the course. This training allows individuals to take great strides in their personal relationship with God and in ministry. It changes lives in a very simple, yet powerful way.

http://www.zoeministries.org/one-on-one-discipleship/

For more information on courses offered by ZOE Ministries International, please visit the ZOE website at www.zoeministries.org.

LEADER´S GUIDE

LEADER'S GUIDE

Leading others into a deeper relationship with God is close to the Father's heart! May He enable you to communicate His love to the members of your group.

Time Frame

Even though each series is designed to last six weeks, you may extend the study as needed. For *Who Is Jesus?*, we suggest you allow about an hour for your group to proceed through the readings and to share their answers to the questions. The first three lessons of *Who Is God the Father?* should last about an hour as well. For the latter half of *Who Is God the Father?* and all of *Who Is the Holy Spirit?*, you will find it necessary to allow up to 1½ hours. More time may be needed for your meeting if reading the Bible is a new skill for participants.

Study Materials

The materials that participants need for this study include a Bible and a copy of this Study Guide. When a lesson has separate versions for the participant and the facilitator, you will lead the lesson from the Facilitator's Version.

If the members of your small group are not familiar with the Bible, you may want to distribute identical versions of the Bible. Then, as you find the assigned passage, you can refer them to a specific page number. By the time your group begins *Who Is the Holy Spirit?*, participants are expected to bring their own Bible. The material covered in the three series, *Who Is Jesus?*, *Who Is God the Father?*, *Who Is the Holy Spirit?*, progressively becomes more complex. This is one reason why we recommend that you complete the series in the suggested order.

Class Format

Greet Group Members

Personally greet each person as they arrive. As facilitator, you want to create an atmosphere of joy, caring and acceptance. Remember that the joy of the Lord is your strength (Nehemiah 8:10). The more comfortable people are, the more they will participate in the discussions. Be sure the meeting location is conducive to discussion and learning.

Distribute Class Materials

Distribute Bibles at the beginning of each lesson. Participants should bring their Study Guide to each meeting. If participants don't have their own Study Guide, hand out copies of the pages with questions. Provide pens or pencils for those who want to write answers in their Study Guide.

Open With Prayer

After study materials have been distributed, open the lesson with a short, simple prayer. You are serving as a model for praying aloud in a small group setting. In later lessons as the group becomes comfortable with the format and with each other, you might want to ask a participant ahead of time to open the lesson with a short prayer.

Lead the Discussion

Begin the discussion time by asking a participant to read aloud the opening paragraph(s). The more participants are given the chance to speak or read, the more likely they will share during the discussion.

Pose the questions in the lesson. If there is a Facilitator's Version of the lesson, use that version. Notice the answers in italics, provided after each question. When possible, ask participants to read the Bible verses. Allow people time to absorb the meaning of the scripture and to formulate an answer. You may want to repeat or rephrase the question. Periods of silence are acceptable.

If someone gives an unscriptural answer, acknowledge that you heard him. See if another participant has a differing view. Ask,

"What does someone else think about that?" The idea is to encourage participation. As people share from their heart, you will understand how to pray for them during the week. If you discern that further discussion with a participant is warranted, you may want to speak with that person privately after class.

Use eye contact and body language to encourage comments from quiet people and to control monopolizers. People will not want to return if one person talks too much. If necessary, speak to a monopolizer in private, enlisting his help in drawing out the quieter participants.

Above all, be sensitive to participants. Make them feel welcome and accepted for who they are. Listen to what they are saying and not saying. Ask God to help you see them as He sees them.

Some lessons include a time for participants to deepen their commitment to the Lord. The "Introduction" page that begins each series will alert you to those special lessons. Allow enough time in that lesson for interested participants to make that commitment.

Try to end each lesson on time. Participants will be more comfortable coming next time if you end on time.

Close With Prayer

Close the lesson with a short, simple prayer related to the lesson, e.g., in *Who Is Jesus*, Lesson 1, you might pray, "Jesus, help us value what is eternal more than what is not eternal. Help us desire a close relationship with you more than possessions or status. Amen."

Importance of Prayer

As facilitator, it is important that you pray for each participant between lessons, remembering that God is the One who draws participants into a deeper relationship with Him. Ask the Lord to reveal Himself to participants and to enable them to receive His love for them (Ephesians 1:17–19; 3:16–21). May He fill you with His love for each participant and show you how to pray for each one.

Special Opportunity Lessons

During each of the three series, participants are offered the opportunity to accept Jesus Christ as their Lord and Savior. Lesson 6 in *Who Is Jesus?*, Lesson 4 in *Who Is God the Father?* and Lesson 5 in *Who Is the Holy Spirit?* all contain the wording you may use to lead interested participants in a prayer of salvation. Lesson 5 of *Who Is the Holy Spirit?* also provides participants the opportunity to be filled with the Holy Spirit.

WHO IS JESUS?
Facilitator's Version

1. "In the beginning was the Word, and the Word was with God, and the Word was God. He was with God in the beginning. Through Him all things were made; without Him nothing was made that has been made."
   John 1:1–3

   "In the beginning God created the heavens and the earth ...Then God said, 'Let us make man in our image, in our likeness... .' "
   Genesis 1:1, 26

   John 1:2 refers to a person ("**He**"). Who was with God in the beginning? What else do we learn from these verses?

   (This Person was involved with God in creation, is the Word, and is God.)

2. **"...in whom we have redemption, the forgiveness of sins. He is the image of the invisible God, the firstborn over all creation. For by Him all things were created... ."** *Colossians 1:14–16*

    This verse also refers to Jesus Christ as being involved in creation. What else do we learn about Jesus?

    (Jesus Christ is the one who brings salvation, or redemption, and forgiveness of sins.)

3. **"The Word became flesh and made His dwelling among us. We have seen His glory, the glory of the One and Only, who came from the Father, full of grace and truth."** *John 1:14*

    One of the names of Jesus is **"the Word."** Why is He called that? What does it mean?

    (The term word here is defined as a "divine expression or communication of the inward thoughts and feelings of God.")

    How is Jesus the divine expression or communication of the inward thoughts and feelings of God?

    (Jesus revealed who the Father is, what the Father is like. In fact, according to the book of **Colossians, "He is the image of the invisible God.")**

4. The Bible is called the Word of God. Compare these verses about Jesus, the Word, with the verses about the Word of God.

    "In Him [Jesus] was life, and that life was the light of men. The light shines in the darkness, but the darkness has not understood it." *John 1:4–5*

    "Jesus answered, 'I am the way and the truth and the life. No one comes to the Father except through me.' " *John 14:6*

"For the word of God is living and active."   *Hebrews 4:12*

How is Jesus like the Word of God in these verses?

(Both have life.)

5. Now compare these verses about Jesus and the Word of God.

"When Jesus spoke again to the people, He said, 'I am the light of the world. Whoever follows me will never walk in darkness, but will have the light of life.' "   *John 8:12*

"Your [God's] word is a lamp to my feet and a light for my path."   *Psalm 119:105*

How is Jesus like the Word of God in these verses?

(Both provide light.)

6. Some people assume that Jesus wrote the Scriptures, the Bible, but that is not true.

"Above all, you must understand that no prophecy of Scripture came about by the prophet's own interpretation. For prophecy never had its origin in the will of man, but men spoke from God as they were carried along by the Holy Spirit."   *2 Peter 1:20–21*

"All Scripture is God-breathed... ."   *2 Timothy 3:16*

According to these verses, who did write the Scriptures?

(Men wrote Scripture, the Bible, as they were inspired or guided by God through the Holy Spirit. This is why the Word of God is infallible—without error and dependable.)

Jesus said, "Heaven and earth will pass away, but my words will never pass away" (Matthew 24:35). See Matthew 5:18

and **Psalms 119:89** for further study.

7. Why do you think that the Bible is difficult to understand at times?

    (God is spirit and His Word nourishes our spirit. Our minds, however, may struggle with the Word of God.)

    "This is what we speak, not in words taught us by human wisdom but in words taught by the Spirit, expressing spiritual truths in spiritual words. The man without the Spirit does not accept the things that come from the Spirit of God, for they are foolishness to him, and he cannot understand them, because they are spiritually discerned."
    1 Corinthians 2:13–14

8. Why do you think the Bible was written?

    "But these are written that you may believe that Jesus is the Christ, the son of God, and that by believing you may have life in His name."
    John 20:31

    (This verse is pretty clear.)

    Do you have any questions about how you can receive the gift of life Jesus offers? Would you like to consider receiving Jesus Christ right now? I would be glad to help you.

    For those who are interested, lead them in a prayer like the one below.

    Dear Jesus Christ,

    I am sorry for the things I have done wrong in my life. Please forgive me. I now turn from everything I know is wrong.

    Thank you for dying on the cross for me so that I could be forgiven and be set free. Thank you for

offering me forgiveness and the gift of your Spirit. I now receive those gifts.

Please come into my life by your Holy Spirit, to be with me forever. Be my leader, forgiver and friend, Amen.

Other resources by ZOE Ministries International

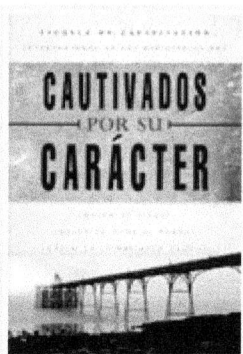

DO YOU KNOW A SPANISH SPEAKER WHO MIGHT LIKE TO KNOW GOD?

Captivated by Their Character is now available in Spanish as Cautivados por su Carácter. (Now also available in French). Go to contact@zoemin.org for details.

Others can come to know the three Persons of the Trinity and how they uniquely relate to us. Help them see how amazing Jesus is! Enable them to feel the love of God the Father for them. Watch the Holy Spirit transform their lives!

- Give your Spanish-speaking friends the gift of a personal relationship with the Lord.

- Send multiple copies of this valuable Bible Study series to a Spanish-speaking missionary you know.

- Use this book to reach out to Spanish-speaking neighbors.

- Recommend this book to a Spanish-speaking church in your city.

After completing these lessons on the Trinity, hopefully they will be captivated by Their character!

For a book description in Spanish, go to:
www.cautivados.com

www.ingramcontent.com/pod-product-compliance
Lightning Source LLC
Chambersburg PA
CBHW060724030426

42337CB00017B/3005